A Devoted
Collective
Compilation

# PRAYERS FOR A GENERATION

Standing in
the Gap for
the Rising
Generations

# The DEVOTED Collective

The Devoted Collective
Auckland, New Zealand
www.thedevotedcollective.org

ISBN Hardcover 978-0-473-59554-8

Cover design by Holly Robertson

Edited by Ellie Di Julio and Aimée Walker

Cataloguing in Publishing Data Title: Prayers for a Generation
Author: The Devoted Collective
Subjects: Devotions, Christian life, Spirituality

A copy of this title is held at the National Library of New Zealand

For the rising generations. We declare
you will be mighty in the land; the
generation of the upright will be blessed.
*Psalm 112:2*

# CONTENTS

# INTRODUCTION

I became a step-mother when I was nineteen. Basically a child myself, I struggled in my new role. I didn't know how to parent a six-year-old, and I certainly didn't know how to cope with the resentment surging in both our hearts as we learned to share the most important man in our lives. Desperate for the dynamic in our relationship to change, I purchased a copy of Stormie Omartian's "The Power of a Praying Parent." As I began to work my way through it, something profound happened: The Lord gave me a mother's heart for my step-daughter, allowing me to see her through His eyes. Resentment gave way to understanding, and I began to feel a fierce protectiveness for her as the Lord frequently placed her on my heart to pray for. We've navigated much together over the years, and I'm grateful to say this love God gave me has held firm. She's now twenty-six, and I no longer use the word 'step' in relation to her—she is my daughter, and wonderfully, now she is grown, also my friend.

Prior to this, I had believed that prayer was not my 'spiritual gift,' and therefore, not my responsibility; I could safely leave this task to the intercessors, the ones who seem to have a direct line to heaven. But God used the experience with my eldest daughter to awaken me to the power of prayer and to teach me that it is the responsibility of *every* believer. When I later became a biological mother, Omartian's book continued to help me to be faithful to this assignment, teaching me how to allow God's Word to shape my prayers and be the truth that I declared over my children. Her writing impacted me so profoundly that her book became a favourite to gift new mothers—more than nappies and cute outfits, what they really need is to know how to pray for their children.

Nothing has driven me to my knees more than the responsibility of motherhood; parenting has been both a beautiful and profoundly painful journey for me. In addition to blending a family, I have experienced the grief of miscarriage, the heartbreak of fostering, and the trauma of supporting a child with mental illness. And through all the highs and lows of raising children, "on your knees" has been the Lord's repeated instruction to me. Despite witnessing firsthand the miraculous ways He works through our prayers, I often need to be reminded that the wisdom I long for and the solutions my family needs can only be found in conversation with Him.

In 2020, those words reached a crescendo. With the world as we had known it crumbling before our eyes and one of our children firmly in the grip of depression, I quickly reached the end of what earthly comfort and wisdom could offer. I knew the Lord was calling me into a season of more intentional prayer—for myself, yes, and also for my children, but more than that, He was expanding my heart to beat for *all* children to know and love God, their only true hope in seemingly hopeless times.

Alongside "on your knees," then, the Lord began to speak a new word: 'mother.' You have to know that, although I am the adoring mother of four children, I am not really a kid person, so this word didn't immediately resonate with me. Yet the Spirit continued to whisper 'mother' during times of corporate worship or while I was driving around carloads of youth; rather than being put off by teen behaviour, my heart would ache for their brokenness. Just like the shift in my heart for my eldest daughter was a work of the Spirit, so too was the expansion of my heart to embrace an entire generation.

My obedience to this renewed call to intercession started with writing out small portions of Psalm 119 each morning, turning its verses into prayers for my family. Later, I began to post the prayers I wrote to social media, inviting others to pray with me and raise a shield of faith for all the young people in our lives. I did not want to sit by idly and allow the enemy to rob our children of what God had intended for them. Little did I know that these prayers would become the seeds of a new movement as others penned their own prayers, lending their voices and strength to the project.

Matthew Arnold once wrote, "If there ever comes a time when the women of the world come together purely and simply for the benefit of mankind, it will be a force such as the world has never known." If this is true of women's earthly power, it is even more true when God's daughters, who have access to the throne room of Heaven, stand together, united in prayer and Kingdom purpose. The world may feel messy and hard at times, but we are not powerless in the face of the enemy's attempts to steal, kill, and destroy the faith of our children. We are here for such a time as this. We carry solutions for our families and for the nations, and our prayers have the power to change the trajectory of entire generations, shaping their hearts and lives for the Father's glory.

In Ezekiel 22, we read of a time in Israel's history when they had rebelled against the Lord. We're told that God looked for someone who would build up Jerusalem's protective wall and stand before Him in the gap on behalf of the land in order to spare them from the destruction their sin warranted—but He found no one (v. 30). This must not be the case for the rising generations. When they are unable or unwilling to fortify their own 'walls,' we must arise to stand in the gap for them, pouring our prayers into their broken places, putting ourselves between them and the enemy's schemes, and believing for them to encounter the ultimate gap-filler, Jesus, so that they can receive mercy and grace in place of the judgment their sins deserve. Standing in the gap is not solely the territory of 'mothers,' but of all believers, regardless of gender or role. Whether you are a teacher, youth leader, relative, or friend, you can arise, taking up your authority in Christ to fight where the true battle lies: in the Heavenly realms.

To help you do this, we've collated forty prayers, written by women across the globe, and paired them with devotional pieces to stir you to focused intercession and Scriptures to personalise and pray over the children you carry in your heart. Each prayer is carefully grounded in the truth of God's

Word and meant to be read aloud; there is power in aligning ourselves with Scripture and in making it our confession. Proverbs 7:3 exhorts us to write God's commandments and teachings on the tablet of our heart; one of the ways that we can do this is through declaring Scripture. There is something that transpires when we speak the Word and 'hear' it that causes faith to be ignited within us (Romans 10:17). I urge you to take the time to look up the Scriptures referenced at the end of each prayer—read them aloud, insert the names of the children you're interceding for, allow your mind to be renewed and your faith to be activated. Know that His Word is true and that it always produces fruit, accomplishing His will and prospering everywhere He sends it (Isaiah 55:11).

Whether you incorporate this book into your quiet time, use it to facilitate an intentional period of prayer, or find yourself reaching for it in the night watches, our hope is that this collection of prayers equips and encourages you to stand in the gap not only for your own children but for a whole generation as they navigate this world and their journey with the Lord.

Agreeing with you for a generation to know and love Him with wholehearted devotion,

Aimée Walker
*Founder, The Devoted Collective*

PRAYERS FOR A GENERATION

# 01
## IN YOUR STRENGTH

*Aimée Walker*

Of all the things I want for my children, the thing I want most is Jesus. I want them to know and love Him. I want them to know the truth of who He is, to experience His freedom, and behold His beauty. I want them to walk in the abundance of all He is and all He has promised. I want to know their futures are secure for all eternity.

But sometimes this desire feels so heavy. I worry that I haven't done enough; I fear failing at training them in the way that they should go (Proverbs 22:6). Anxiety creeps in for their futures, and I find myself working overtime to rescue and protect them from all the things.

God frequently has to remind me that, as much as I want Jesus for my children, it's not my job to *be* Jesus. I am not and cannot be their Saviour. That job has been taken and I do not need to carry that weight. And neither do you.

Sometimes, to effectively pray for our children, we must first pray for our own hearts. It's important that in our desperation for them to know God that we do not stand in the gap in our own strength or wisdom but in His. As Paul exhorts us, we must learn to be strong in the Lord and in His mighty power (Ephesians 6:10)—that is the only way we can stand firm against the enemy's attempts to steal the hope of Jesus from this generation.

Father, we bring ourselves before You today. You know the children that we carry in our hearts and the weight that we feel for their salvation. We release them to You today, Lord, and we ask that You do what we cannot. Teach us how to stand firm in Your strength and in Your mighty power. We believe that You have trained our hands for this battle, equipping us to take our stand against the enemy's schemes. We commit to be faithful in prayer, praying in the Spirit and trusting in His ability to convict, instruct, and lead our children into all truth. As we stand in the gap, may we do so with hope, joy, and grace, knowing that, in Christ, we are more than conquerors. In Jesus' name, Amen.

—— SCRIPTURES TO PRAY ——

Psalm 18:34-35, 144:1
John 16:8-15
Ephesians 6:10-20

# 02
## KNOW THE TRUTH
*Aimée Walker*

One of the greatest lies that's been sold to this generation is that truth is relative. Once preceded by a simple 'the,' the word 'truth' is far more likely to follow 'my' or 'your' these days. Grammar may not be exciting, but it matters. Switching from a definite article to a possessive adjective insinuates ownership over truth, as though it is something that can shift and change from person to person, something an individual has the power to determine. But truth, by its very nature is objective, and ultimately, as believers, we know truth is a person. Truth is Jesus.

In John 14:6, Jesus declares, "I am the way, the truth, and the life…." Earlier, in John 8:33, He says that those who know the truth will be set free. Yes, intimate knowledge of Jesus Christ as the unchanging truth is what our hearts need if we are to walk in the freedom God intended for us.

God impressed this upon me strongly during a time of intercession for one of my children when He gave me Psalm 51:6 to pray over them: "Surely You desire truth in the inmost being; You teach me wisdom in the inmost place" (BSB). These words have continued to resound in my spirit not only for my child, but for a generation entangled in the enemy's deception. Our children need a revelation of Jesus—they need to know the truth of who He is in their innermost being.

And so do we. As parents, we also need the hope, the strength, the life, and the wisdom that only Jesus holds if we are to raise a generation to stand firm in truth. It starts with us. It starts with being willing to yield to His authority and to model to our children the power and freedom that flows from submitting to it.

Father, we know that You desire truth to reign within us. We invite You now to dismantle the lies we have believed and to teach us wisdom in our inmost places that we might disciple a generation and reveal to them the truth of Jesus. Let us demonstrate His beauty, His strength, His hope, and His life to them with integrity of heart. Let us walk in Your freedom so they might, too. We bring our children before You and ask that, just as You instruct us, You would instruct them. Tear down the lies and strongholds that prevent them from recognising Jesus and establish Your truth in their hearts and minds. Teach them, Lord, that their peace might be great. We ask these things In Jesus' name, *Amen.*

—— SCRIPTURES TO PRAY ——

Psalm 51:6
Isaiah 54:13
John 8:32, 14:6
2 Corinthians 10:4-5

# 03
## GIVE THEM ENCOUNTERS
*Hannah Tan*

My husband and I have been watching *The Chosen*, a historical fiction TV series based on the life of Jesus. Over and over, we see people from the Gospels encounter Him. They meet Him in the midst of their ordinary days, often desperate for healing, acceptance, or change. The disciples, the woman at the well, the lepers, the blind, the oppressed and marginalised—all are transformed by their encounters with Jesus. By the time they walk away, they each know in the depths of their soul that Jesus is real and that He loves them and sees them. And no one can take that testimony away.

Watching these stories unfold, I keep coming back to a turning point in my own life when I was set free of my fear, healed in my mind, and had my financial situation redeemed all at once. In that one moment, I knew I was seen, loved, found, saved, and called by name—because of Jesus. This is my testimony, and I have needed its encouragement through all the life storms that have followed since.

One thing I pray this generation will have is their own touchstone encounter with Jesus. That our kids would have a testimony of his love, healing, grace at work in their lives. That when doubts and hardships come, they can look back on that one moment and know God loves them, sees them, is for them, and is at work in their lives—even now—because He never changes.

Father, we thank you for showing Your great love for us through Jesus. Thank You for revealing, through the Gospels, that we are never too hidden or too broken for You to know our names or to show us how much Your heart is towards us. Father, we ask that our children would have a powerful encounter with You—a defining moment when nothing else matters but that they are seen and loved and called by name. No matter what circumstances they find themselves in, we pray they would look to You and remember Your presence in their lives—Your call, encouragement, and care. Thank You for Your faithfulness to give a new generation these testimonies as You have done for us and generations past.

In Jesus' name, Amen.

—— SCRIPTURES TO PRAY ——

John 3:16-17
Romans 8:27-28
Hebrews 13:8
Revelation 12:11

# 04
## TURN OUR HEARTS
*Aimée Walker*

"You just don't understand!" As a parent, I'm frequently on the receiving end of those words, but I well remember when I was the one yelling them. At the time, I truly believed my mother couldn't possibly understand my world; now I realise how much she likely did and how often I robbed myself of her wisdom and insight.

At some point, every generation feels the weight of the gap between themselves, those who have gone before, and those who are coming after. Things get lost in translation, and labels seek to divide and define us. We feel misunderstood, cut off from one another by generational battle lines. But Jesus came to usher in a different way—a turning of hearts towards one another.

The prophet Malachi foretold the coming of John the Baptist, prophesying that he would turn the hearts of fathers to their children and the hearts of children to their fathers so that they could be a people ready and prepared for the Lord (Malachi 4:5-6). Not only that, but as the hearts of fathers were turned toward their children, so, too, would the disobedient be enabled to receive the wisdom of the righteous (Luke 1:17). As the generations unite, there is a softening of hearts toward the message of the Kingdom of God.

The Father desires strong and healthy generational ties— that young and old would come together in understanding, lending their strength to one another to show the world the power and the beauty of family. He wants this to be true both in our homes and in our churches. He longs for the body of Christ, the family of God, to model the culture of Heaven and be a place where all generations are honoured as they turn not only toward God but also to each other.

Father, we thank You for Your heart for family and for Your desire to bestow honour on every generation. We thank You that in Christ there is a place of value for each of us; that there is room for every generation to grow and thrive and contribute to Your Kingdom; and that the old dream dreams, the young see visions, and our children prophesy. We ask by the power of Your Spirit that You would turn our hearts toward one another, breaking down the walls of generational divide and misunderstanding to restore honour to Your House and to our homes. Give us wisdom as fathers and mothers to not provoke and frustrate the younger generations but to connect their hearts to Yours so that the blessing of walking in Your ways might pass from generation to generation.

In Jesus' name, Amen.

—— SCRIPTURES TO PRAY ——

Malachi 4:5-6
Luke 1:17
Acts 2:17
Ephesians 6:4

## 05

## SOFTEN HEARTS AND TONGUES

*Lori Ann Wood*

I lost my momma this past year. The worst part is I can't talk to her anymore. I think about the times in high school I purposefully gave her the silent treatment, instinctively knowing that it was the most powerful weapon I had, the way to hurt her most—even worse than the heated arguments. Now as a mom with my own young adults, I know this to be true. Difficult as they are, debates and disagreements are where our bond is forged; the times my children are quiet are the times my heart breaks because I am locked out of their lives.

Vocalised strife doesn't kill a relationship; silent indifference does.

Father God understands this need for communication. Entire books of the Bible are dedicated to difficult discussions: Job, Psalms, Lamentations, and Ecclesiastes, for example. Both David, the man after God's own heart, and Jesus, the Man who embodied it, talked to God in honest, sometimes uncomfortable terms. David—dismissed, hunted, and rejected—penned nearly half of the Psalms, asking "How long? Why? Where are You?" Centuries later, Jesus pleaded for answers in Gethsemane before His crucifixion—"Remove this cup" (Luke 22:42)—and at Golgotha in the middle of it— "Why have You forsaken Me?" (Matthew 27:46). When the hard parenting path calls my conflict-averse self to silence, I want to follow their example: to encourage my children to voice their feelings and to do the same with my Father.

Rather than running from the struggle, I hope my children can be open with me, just as God longs for us to bring our truest emotions to Him. After all, if David and Jesus are any indication, emotional honesty is one of the best ways to build a solid relationship, even if it is loud or messy.

I'm fairly certain Mom would agree.

Father God, thank You for Your example of how to grow closer to each other and to You, even in times of strife and confusion. Thank You for Your gift of all-consuming grace as we question and stumble, argue and wander, both as parents and as children. As You teach us in Your Word, when we forge deeper into difficult conversations, we venture deeper into the hearts of our children and they into ours. Keep us constantly communicating, longing for rich relationship with You and with each other. Soften their hearts as you soften our tongues. Give us all courage to face future discussions and resilience to reconcile past ones. Stay near as we walk these difficult, sometimes foreign paths of parenting. And even in times of silence with You and with them, may Your Spirit keep our bond alive.
In Jesus' name, Amen.

—— SCRIPTURES TO PRAY ——

Psalm 10:1, 13:1-6
Ecclesiastes 1:1-11, 12:13-14
Matthew 27:46-50
Luke 22:42-44

# 06
## RAISE UP JONATHANS
*Aimée Walker*

It was my first day at a new school, and I was nervous. Wanting to encourage me, my poppa took me over to a framed embroidery hanging on my grandparents' kitchen wall that read: "To have a friend you must be a friend." The words have stuck with me ever since.

I want my kids to be great friends; I want them to be loyal, trustworthy, and kind. But I also want them to *have* great friends—friends who sharpen and hone them, who help them guard their hearts, who draw out the best in them. I want each of them to have at least one 'Jonathan' in their life and to be Jonathan to someone else.

If you're wondering what I mean by this, take a look at 1 Samuel 18 and 20. Jonathan was the son of King Saul and the rightful heir to the throne God had promised to David, yet rather than being threatened by David, Jonathan "loved him as his own soul" (1 Samuel 18:3) and was a faithful friend. Jonathans do not see themselves as being in competition with others; they are secure in who they are and what God is calling them to do, and this security releases them to champion the people around them. They encourage, equip, and call forth the God-given destiny in the people they love, even when circumstances seem to oppose it.

These are the friends I want for my kids—and the friends I want them to be for others—so that community can be for them the source of joy and strength God intended it to be.

Father, we bring our children before You and ask that You would give them discernment to choose their friends well. Protect them from relationships that could corrupt their character and surround them with friends who will stick closer than a brother, who will sharpen them as iron sharpens iron so they can walk in the fullness of all that You have created and purposed them for. Raise up Jonathans to champion the call upon their lives and enable them to do this for others. Help them to wear Your love at all times and to be secure in their value as Your child so they can freely demonstrate Your love and grace to those around them. In Jesus' name, Amen.

—— SCRIPTURES TO PRAY ——

Proverbs 12:26, 18:24, 27:17
1 Corinthians 15:33
Colossians 3:12-14

# 07
## SPEAK LIFE
*Aimée Walker*

I was once invited to be part of a series on the Proverbs 31 woman. I was given the topic of wisdom and was so excited to dive into preparing my message—until I read the specific verse they'd assigned me: "She speaks with wisdom, and faithful instruction is on her tongue..." (v. 26). I inwardly groaned. *Why did it have to mention our tongues?*

In my current stage of parenting, I am acutely aware of the power of words. Living in the age of social media adds another whole layer of complexity to not only the messages our children are absorbing but also to how they and their friends are communicating. Misunderstandings are perpetuated by short responses void of tone or facial expressions, and things are said hiding behind screens that would never be said face to face.

Proverbs says our words are like deep waters for good reason (18:4); they can sweep us away, straight into danger. *Is there anything that gets us in as much trouble as the words we speak? Anything that hurts as much as the words others speak to us?*

But the same verse in Proverbs also tells us that "the fountain of wisdom is a rushing stream." Unlike deep waters, where we can find ourselves over our heads, streams are a source of life. My prayer is that God would raise up our children to be a voice—a gushing stream—of life to their generation; a voice that will point the way to Jesus, who is Living Water to their souls.

Father, from the beginning of Scripture we see the power of the spoken word. You spoke, and it was. We pray that You would impress upon our children the power of their own words—that they would recognise with every word they speak that they can create life or destruction. Help them to store up Your truth in their hearts that they might speak with wisdom; grow in them the fruit of self-control to weigh their words carefully; and fill them with Your love by the power of Your Holy Spirit so their words can bring healing. Let streams of Living Water well up within them and overflow to their generation that all might know You. In Jesus' name, Amen.

—— SCRIPTURES TO PRAY ——

Psalm 141:3
Proverbs 12:18-19, 18:4, 21:23
Luke 6:45

# 08
## MADE IN YOUR IMAGE
*Vicki Bentley*

I watched with pride as my six-year-old daughter mingled with the eclectic group of people in attendance at our church's community outreach event. As a child on the autism spectrum, her 'atypical' communication skills can often present challenges in social situations. But not this time. Uninhibited and unfiltered, I saw her welcome people with exuberance, finding a way to break down barriers, make people smile, and show love to a hurting community—just by being herself.

The world isn't always kind to our precious children who don't fit the mold, those who sing their own melodies and dance to the beat of their own drum. Their differences can set them apart—in all the 'wrong' ways—and they often find themselves marginalised, ostracised, and under relentless pressure to conform to others expectations and standards.

Thankfully, God has a different perspective. He has created these children in His image, after all. They're His masterpiece, designed for good works He has prepared for them in advance (Ephesians 2:10). In view of this, their differences can and should be celebrated as distinct reflections of who God is, providing them with opportunities to impact His Kingdom and to draw people to Him in ways that others simply cannot.

It is our job to remind our children daily of who God says they are instead of all that the world says they are not; to empower and encourage and advocate for and delight in them; to let their beautiful light shine instead of unconsciously snuffing it out in our desire for them to 'fit in.' But ultimately, our job is to point them to Jesus—then watch as He works in and through them in ways we couldn't possibly imagine.

Father God, we pray that our children would see themselves the way You do. Help them to know that no matter how they 'measure up' to the standards of this world, they are created first and foremost in Your image—fearfully and wonderfully with a divinely-appointed plan and purpose. Thank You that their unique gifts and personalities reflect wonderfully different facets of who You are. Help us to celebrate this uniqueness and to be their biggest cheerleader and advocate in a world that may not always appreciate them as they are. Above all, help us to point them toward You to find their true identity and worth in You alone. In Jesus' name, Amen.

—— SCRIPTURES TO PRAY ——

Psalm 139:13-18
Jeremiah 1:5, 29:11
Ephesians 2:10
Romans 12:4-6 (MSG)

## 09
## FAN INTO FLAME
*Aimee Walker*

Looking back on my childhood, two great loves emerged early on: the Church and writing. Yet for some reason, I never considered either of them when contemplating what to do with my life. In fact, I never really stopped to consider who I truly was nor did I pray about what God might be inviting me to do. This allowed others and the culture around me to shape my trajectory, and consequently, a sense of restlessness ensued. It took me a long time to discover who God created me to be and how my lifelong passions fit in.

This experience has enabled me to spot the same happening in my children. Watching them grow and discover their own passions, I can see how the enemy employs two key tactics when it comes to our gifting: he outright attacks it, attempting to destroy who God has fashioned and called us to be, or he subtly tries to distract us and cause us to forget or lose sight of that calling.

Throughout Paul's first letter to Timothy, the apostle exhorts his young apprentice to fan into flame the gift which is in him (2 Timothy 1:6). As I think about my children and the generation coming through, I want to be a woman who sees their potential, recognises the call of God upon their lives, and helps them fan it into flame. I want to be a mother who lifts up a shield of faith to ward off the attacks of the enemy on their destiny. I want to help them walk in the fullness of all God has planned for them by reminding them not only of their identity in Christ but also of their purpose.

Father, we thank You that each of us is fearfully and wonderfully made—a unique masterpiece created anew in Christ to do the good works You have prepared for us. We pray that we would recognise and walk in the giftings You have placed within our lives and also to recognise them in others. Help us to fan into flame the spiritual gifts You have placed within our children by creating a culture where they can discover who they are in Christ and grow into maturity so they can serve You well. We lift up a shield of faith for this generation, refusing to allow the enemy to steal, kill, or destroy on our watch. We declare that no weapon formed against them will prosper but that Your Word will accomplish the purpose for which You sent it in their lives.

In Jesus' name, *Amen.*

—— SCRIPTURES TO PRAY ——

Psalm 139:13-16
Isaiah 54:17, 55:11
John 10:10
Ephesians 2:10
2 Timothy 1:6

# 10
## CAPTIVATE THEM, JESUS

*Rebecca Brand*

We live in a time where it has never been easier to voice our opinions and have others from all around the world hear them. Yet, the pressures within this are monumental, and mental illness, identity crises, and suicide rates are at alarming highs because of this overwhelming desire to be seen, heard, and valued.

On one hand, this rising generation is powerfully influenced by social media, but on the other, I see a ripening about to occur, a harvest that is ready to be gathered. Naturally, the enemy is trying his best to distract and disarm this rising army. We must pray that those schemes would fail and that their attention would instead be captivated by Jesus.

In John 4, we meet the 'woman at the well.' Rejected by society for living in sin and ostracised for her past choices, her life is transformed when she encounters Jesus. He knows her story, and yet without judgment He draws her attention beyond the here and now to the glorious future ruled by the Spirit (vv.23-24), allowing her to understand that He is a Prophet and the long-awaited Messiah.

I love that Jesus speaks to the day when true worshippers will worship in Spirit and truth, because it allows her to focus on what could be rather than her current circumstances. No wonder she drops her water jar and rushes back to her village to share what has happened with everyone! As she learns from Jesus, she takes up the mantle of evangelism on her life, overthrowing the constraints society has placed upon her. The revelation of Jesus and renewed hope make her rise up with boldness.

*How incredible would it be to see the next generation full of faith and courage, stepping into the callings and giftings God has placed upon them? To see them walking in divine purpose by listening not to the voices around them but to Christ's?* What greater things could they do then (John 14:12)!

Father, we thank You that there is no condemnation in Christ—that in Your grace You have removed our sin from us and now invite us to participate in the life of the Kingdom. We pray that there will no longer be any fear in the hearts of the rising generation; that they will know You have given them a Spirit of love, power, and a sound mind to conquer not only the deepest valleys of judgement but also to stay close to You when they reach the mountaintops. Father, allow this generation to be rooted in Christ, looking to Him alone for purpose and validation. By Your Spirit empower them to act justly, love mercy, and walk humbly with You as they pursue 'greater things' for Your glory. In Jesus' name, *Amen.*

—— SCRIPTURES TO PRAY ——

Micah 6:8
John 4:23-24, 14:12
Romans 8:1
2 Timothy 1:7

# II
## FEAR THE LORD
*Aimée Walker*

The word 'fear' often gets a bad rap. In our desire to be obedient to Scripture's frequent command to "fear not," we can inadvertently buy into the idea that we are being asked to be fear-less, when actually what we are being called to do is to rightly position our fear. The word most commonly used throughout the New Testament for 'fear' is *phobeō*, and it means all the things that you would expect: to frighten, to cause to flee by terrifying, to be afraid. But it also means to be in awe of, to reverence, to venerate. Like a two-sided coin, *phobeō* presents us with a choice: Will fear terrify and shut us down, or will it lead us closer to God?

Scripture is clear: The fear of the Lord is the beginning of wisdom (Proverbs 9:10) and a necessary ingredient to living a life devoted to intimacy with Him. Rightly directed, fear is to our benefit, enabling us to trust and surrender to Christ's Lordship and receive the blessings He has for us.

It's equally clear that, in the absence of the fear of the Lord, sin creeps into our lives; when fear is misdirected, it becomes a tool of the enemy to steal, kill, and destroy. I've seen this happen far too often in my own children's lives. The fear of man ensnares them, and in their attempts to impress their peers, they aren't always true to themselves or to God; similarly, the fear of 'what if' can stop them from pursuing the things that are in their hearts to be and to do. I long for them to learn to look to the Lord when fear comes knocking so they can experience the abundant life Christ promises to those who follow Him.

Father, as we raise children and mentor generations, we pray for our own fear to be rightly directed. Help us to keep our hearts fixed on You, worshipping You with reverence and with awe, that we might demonstrate the blessing it is to fear the Lord. We thank You that Your eyes are on those who fear You. Your angels encamp around them, and You deliver them; You reward them with riches, honour, wisdom, and life, satisfying them with the fruit of Your hands and instructing them in the way they should choose. May our children and those who follow after them walk in Your ways, fearing You above all else, that all these blessings and more might be theirs. In Jesus' name, Amen.

—— SCRIPTURES TO PRAY ——

Deuteronomy 6:24
Psalm 34:4-11
Proverbs 19:23, 22:4
Isaiah 33:5-6
John 10:10

# 12
## ABOUND IN KNOWLEDGE

*Aimée Walker*

Charles Spurgeon once said, "Discernment is not knowing the difference between right and wrong. It is knowing the difference between right and almost right."

Every day I watch just how much my children need this gift of discernment. Growing up in an age of relativism with an overwhelming amount of information and opinion available at the touch of a button, they need to be able to discern what is right and true from what is "almost right." But more than that, they also need to know what to do in response to the truth—how to allow it to shape their lives in a world where it is often opposed. This can be a struggle for them, as so often when they stand for God's love and truth, they're accused of hatred and bigotry.

In 1 Chronicles, there's a description of the men from the tribe of Issachar that has always stood out to me. We're told that they "understood the times and knew what Israel should do" (12:32). I long for my children to possess this kind of practical wisdom—to not only love the Lord but to "abound more and more in knowledge and depth of insight, so that they may be able to discern what is best and may be pure and blameless for the day of Christ" (Philippians 1:9-10). I want them to not only *know* the truth but to boldly live it out in such a way that witnesses to their generation. Because truth in action will not only bring freedom to *them* but to anyone stuck in bondage.

Father, we thank You for the depth and the riches of wisdom and knowledge that are found in You. Forge in this generation a righteous fear of the Lord that they might walk in the light of Your truth. We thank You that You have promised that if we lack wisdom we can ask and it will be generously given to us. Today we come and ask for wisdom on behalf of our children. By your grace, renew their minds, enable them to test and discern Your will, cause them to abound in knowledge and insight beyond their years, and instruct them on how they are to live in these days. May the beauty of Your truth capture their hearts and minds, and may they know that Jesus is the One they can always rely upon—the unchanging standard of truth.

In Jesus' name, *Amen.*

—— SCRIPTURES TO PRAY ——

1 Chronicles 12:32
Proverbs 1:7
Romans 11:33-12:2
Philippians 1:9-10
James 1:5

# 13
## AWAKEN WONDER

*Ellie Di Julio*

*It starts so early, doesn't it?* The obsession with screens. Even when my daughter was less than a year old, she would automatically focus on the flashing lights and cheerful sounds coming from a TV or phone. Now that she's five, it seems like we're constantly fighting a war of attention.

Screens aren't inherently bad; technology is all about how you use it. The trouble is that kids are increasingly tuning into their screens and tuning out reality, especially when reality is hard to face. It's far easier to live in a world of constant entertainment where you're in control when everything else is not.

But it's not real. And it dulls your sense of wonder.

It's hard to be affected by the awesome and holy reality around you—the crashing ocean, the Milky Way galaxy, tiramisu, giggling babies—when virtual reality is all you interact with. It's hard to care about anything other than yourself when you can rule universes at a whim and block out anything or anyone disagreeable.

It's also hard to feel like a child of God when you're up to your eyeballs in electronics and can't see the gifts your Father is trying to give you. After all, our sense of wonder makes us childlike: *Is anyone truly a child without it?*

My prayer for this digital generation is that they not become jaded by simulated reality. That they would instead lift their eyes and see God as their wondrous Father, becoming more fully His true children and less a product of the modern era's false comfort. May they never be too plugged in to recognise and receive God's everyday miracles.

Father, we thank You that You never run out of amazing things to share with us. Everything that causes us to stop and say "wow" is a reflection of You. I pray that the children raised in this digital era never lose their sense of wonder, never become jaded or inured to the brilliance of the world and life You designed for them. Help them reject culture's enticement to hollow distractions, to recognise their need for Your holy wonder, and to embrace the good things You have in store for them, if only they will look up to see.
In Jesus' name, Amen.

—— SCRIPTURES TO PRAY ——

Psalm 19:1, 66:5
Matthew 18:3
John 17:25-26
Romans 12:2
1 John 2:15

# 14
## CLEAR THE PATH
*Rachel Rodger*

I have a friend who was a New Zealand ice curling champion, which piqued my interest in the game. I discovered the goal is to deliver a round 'stone' as close to the target centre as possible. Crucial to a successful game is the role of the sweeper. When playing on the ice, the sweeper runs ahead of the travelling stone, brushing the ice vigorously to reduce friction, remove loose debris, and prevent unwanted 'curling,' or veering off-course.

In the same way, our prayers for the next generation can help clear a path for them to draw near to Jesus and connect with Him. Many young people are focused on living in the present moment, but as parents, we have the benefit of a few extra decades of life experience and the wisdom God has given us over the years. Looking ahead and being sensitive to the Holy Spirit's prompting, we can intercept the enemy's schemes, dismantle his lies, and push aside the shame and fear he would throw in their way. We can 'sweep' away obstacles as they cast their stone towards the goal of Christ.

We don't need to fully comprehend our children's future calling in advance—we just need to focus on them finding themselves standing in the circle with Jesus. After all, the game of life is much more fun and thrilling when He is at the centre of everything. As Psalm 16:11 says, "You make known to me the path of life; you will fill me with joy in your presence, with eternal pleasures at your right hand." What an incredible promise we can pray for a generation as God calls them to live for Him!

Heavenly Father, thank You that our lives don't have to be boring. Thank You that our children are designed for playfulness and joyful fun. We pray for their hearts to be filled with a desire for closeness with You and that they will discover how easy it is to approach You themselves. Use our prayers to sweep a clear path for them to You. Smooth their way. Remove any cultural myths that hinder them from seeing You. Shut down any attempts by the enemy to trip them up. Dismiss the deceptions and lies that could distract them from their journey towards You. Draw them to Yourself so they will choose to seek and follow You all the days of their lives. In Jesus' name, *Amen.*

—— SCRIPTURES TO PRAY ——

Psalm 16:11
Isaiah 40:3-5
John 12:31-32
James 4:7-8
Jude 1:23-24

# 15
## ESTABLISHED IN LOVE
*Aimée Walker*

My name means 'beloved,' but honestly, it's not an identity I have always found easy to accept. I *definitely* don't always feel loveable. Yet I've come to understand that trusting in God's unfailing love for each one of us is essential to the Christian life. If we are to grow into maturity, we must first believe that we are deeply loved and that nothing can remove that love from us.

The apostle Paul knew this; that's why he prays in Ephesians 3 for us to be rooted and established in Christ's love (v. 17) so that we might be "filled to the measure of all the fullness of God" (v. 19). Without that foundation, we quite simply cannot grow as He intended us to. But the love of God is so vast, so utterly incomprehensible, that Paul also prays we would have power to grasp the extent of it (v. 18). And God, in His infinite grace, answers that prayer through the indwelling of His Holy Spirit, Who continually pours out the love of the Father upon our hearts and lives (Romans 5:5) so that it does not remain a theory but becomes our lived reality.

As we pray for a generation that desperately needs to know this love, may we be reminded afresh of the Father's unstoppable love for us. May we be empowered to demonstrate it to our children so that they, like us, might grow firmly rooted in the lavish love of the Father, Whose name they bear and to Whom they belong (Ephesians 3:15).

.

Father, we thank You today that whether our children are near or far from You, You love them, and like the father of the prodigal son, You watch for them. Thank You that even while they were sinners, You demonstrated Your love for them, allowing Your Son to die that there might be provision for their healing and restoration as children of God. By the power of Your Holy Spirit, give them a revelation of Your unfailing love. Silence the lies of the enemy that they are unlovable and enable them to understand how wide and long and high and deep the love of Christ is so they can live rooted and grounded in it.
In Jesus' name, *Amen.*

—— SCRIPTURES TO PRAY ——

Psalm 52:8
Romans 5:5-8, 8:35-39
Ephesians 3:15-19
1 John 3:1

# 16
## LET THE LIGHT SHINE
*Aimée Walker*

On a day when my mama heart felt particularly heavy, I opened my Scripture colouring book and resumed working on a page that spoke of the rainbow as a sign of God's covenant with the earth. I had chosen it because I desperately needed a reminder of God's faithfulness in a difficult season. As I shaded clouds and stars and olive branches, the opening words of John's gospel kept coming to mind: "The light shines in the darkness and the darkness can never extinguish it" (1:5 NLT). A quiet hope began to fill me as His peace pushed back the fear that had been gnawing at my heart.

Daily bombarded by all that is wrong in the world, it's easy to look around us and despair for the future of our children, but throughout Scripture we see a different story. The destiny of God's people is not destruction but redemption; it is not to be overcome by the darkness but to be enveloped by His light. It is a legacy of blessing.

The Word assures us that our children will be mighty in the land (Psalm 112:2), encouraging us that our work is not in vain nor are our children be doomed to misfortune for we are people blessed by the LORD, and our children, too, will be blessed (Isaiah 65:23 NLT). Yes, though darkness covers the earth, the Lord rises upon us and His glory appears over us (Isaiah 60:2). Because of this, we look forward not with fear but with hope, allowing it to shape our prayers and declarations for our children and our children's children.

Father, we thank You that our work is not in vain; our children are not destined for misfortune because You have promised that the generation of the upright will be blessed. Make us that generation, Lord. Enable us by Your Spirit to walk with You in righteousness and integrity of heart; let Your glory rise upon us that it might rise upon them. Thank You that You show love for a thousand generations to those who love You and obey Your commands. Thank You for the blessing that will rest upon our children and our children's children as we commit to walking with You. We look to the future today, not with fear, but with great hope knowing You can redeem all things. In Jesus' name, Amen.

──── SCRIPTURES TO PRAY ────

Deuteronomy 7:9
Psalm 112:2
Isaiah 60:1-3, 65:23
John 1:5

# 17
## GATHER THEM, LORD
*Kay Gleaves*

I couldn't find him. I looked everywhere! I searched the whole house. I called the neighbours to see if he had gone over to play with their boys or to the park without telling me. But he was nowhere.

My five-year-old son was missing.

*How does one lose their son in their own home?* Panic made my heart race as I thought of all the scenarios and the time that had lapsed while I had been looking. I ran to his room one more time, desperately searching for a clue as to where he might have gone, wondering if it was time to call the police.

And that's when I saw it. A blanket, wedged in the crack between the wall and the mattress. I yanked on it and underneath was a small boy, sound asleep—worn out from an afternoon in the pool.

I sobbed. The panic had been so real, the worry so intense. Yet, he was never lost. He was never missing. He was right there the whole time.

He's thirty now, but I still worry for this man child. And when that happens, my own Heavenly Father swoops in with the comfort this mama of grown kids needs: "Hear the word of the LORD, you nations; proclaim it in distant coastlands: 'He who scattered Israel will gather them and will watch over his flock like a shepherd'" (Jeremiah 31:10).

Friend, He who scattered Israel *knows* where to find them. He knows. And He will watch over them as a loving shepherd.

*Do you feel the comfort, Mama?* Those grown babies aren't lost—He knows where to find them.

Father, we thank You that our children are never out of Your sight. Even when they seem scattered, lost, missing, or wandering, You know exactly where to find them. You not only see them, You know them and love them wildly and audaciously, with mercy and forgiveness in your outstretched arms. Thank You, God, that You are their loving Shepherd, tending and watching over them even when they are out of sight. Help us, God, to lean on that and "proclaim it in distant coastlands" with the confidence that comes from knowing You as our good, good Father. We release our children to Your more than capable hands, knowing that if they are ever lost, You are faithful to find them. In Jesus' name, Amen.

—— SCRIPTURES TO PRAY ——

Psalm 38:15, 139:7
Jeremiah 31:15-16
Romans 8:38-39

# 18
## IMPART TRUTH
*Rachel Rodger*

Have you ever felt you need a translator for your kids? When our children are working through difficult emotions or experiences, they don't always have the understanding or language to express it clearly. Their inner processing can be hidden from us, and sometimes when they do share, it's easy to misunderstand what they are trying to convey.

Thankfully, however, their hearts and minds are discoverable to the Holy Spirit. As King David reminded his son, Solomon, God "understands every desire and every thought" (1 Chronicles 28:9). We can reassure ourselves and our children that even when we don't fully comprehend everything, God does, and He will impart to us His grace and wisdom.

Just as the Holy Spirit knows the heart of your child, He searches God's will for them, too (Romans 8:27). He can reveal to us as parents and caregivers unique prophetic insight into their lives so that we know what to pray for and over them. It might be a word of knowledge, a vivid dream, or a metaphorical image that shows us areas that need attention. We can intercede for them with the direct guidance of the Holy Spirit.

Prophetic prayer is confidently partnering with God in the dismantling of lies and the impartation of truth that comes through His intimate, powerful work in our children's hearts and minds. When we engage in this kind of intercession on their behalf, we may never know what occurred in those moments—what thought God renewed, what emotion God healed, or what perspective God showed them—but what is certain is that, wherever the Holy Spirit is at work, He always brings freedom. As you continue to pray in spirit and in truth, you can expect the hidden work God does to be translated into joy for both you and your children!

Father, thank You that You care for each of our children intimately. You know the desires of their hearts and every one of their thoughts. Foster understanding between us so we can encourage and spur one another on in love. Give us prophetic discernment to know what to pray for this generation and to help them make sense of the experiences they are having. Holy Spirit, open their hearts to seek You and cry out to You for help when they feel trapped or confused. Give them supernatural dreams and encounters that demonstrate You are with them. Let them discover Your endless grace and wisdom. Let them be amazed at the answers You give them and place all their confidence in You. In Jesus' name, Amen.

—— SCRIPTURES TO PRAY ——

1 Samuel 16:7
Jeremiah 33:2-3
Romans 8:27
1 Corinthians 2:9-11

# 19
## HEM THEM IN
*Aimée Walker*

She walked past me in the supermarket aisle, a baby snug against her chest, her hand gently patting their back. I smiled at her as part of me ached for the days when I held my own babies so close and could protect them with my presence. With children ranging in age from six to twenty-six, this is no longer my reality; I can't always be where they are. But as disquieting as this is at times, I've come to understand that the best protection I can offer them is on my knees. My prayers can be with them even when I am not, and their impact is not diminished by the passing of years. And just as prayer is not limited by time or geography, neither is God.

My mama heart finds great comfort in knowing that where they go, God goes. There is nowhere they can escape from His presence (Psalm 139). Even should they choose to make their bed in the depths or attempt to hide in the darkness, nothing about them is hidden from the Lord. He is the One who formed them and who Has foreseen all of their days. He is always with them, always for them, always working on their behalf and commanding angels to guard over them in all of their ways (Psalm 91:11). Although at times it might seem to us that nothing is happening, His Spirit is proactively ministering to their hearts, seeking their salvation and their sanctification.

As our children grow and can no longer be contained by our arms, we can hold them with our prayers, entrusting their steps to the One who loves them even more than we do.

Father, we thank You for Your hand upon our children. Thank You that You hem them in with Your love and that there is nowhere they can go to escape from Your presence. We ask that You would bless them and keep them, that Your face would be turned toward them, and that they would know the blessing of being at peace with You. Command Your angels concerning them to guard them in all of their ways, and lead them not into temptation, but deliver them from evil that they might walk in the fullness of all You have planned and purposed for them.

In Jesus' name, Amen.

—— SCRIPTURES TO PRAY ——

Numbers 6:24-26
Psalm 91, 139
Matthew 6:9-13

# 20
## PEACE BE WITH YOU

*Aimée Walker*

Filled with fear after the death of their teacher, the disciples had retreated from the world and locked themselves in a room. But then the resurrected Jesus appears to them and not once, but twice, says, "Peace be with you" (John 20:19). As He makes this declaration, their fear gives way to joy. *Why?* Because they have seen the Lord.

We live in uncertain times, and many of us find ourselves hemmed in by fear. Yet Jesus speaks these words to us still: "Peace I leave with you; my peace I give you. I do not give to you as the world gives. Do not let your hearts be troubled and do not be afraid" (John 14:27).

The peace that God gives to us is more than a fleeting feeling. It is His all-encompassing *shalom* blessing; it is wholeness. When we place faith in Jesus Christ—when we believe that His death and resurrection was enough to reconcile us to the Father—that state of being at peace with God is meant to permeate and transform every aspect of our being, bringing wholeness to our bodies, our minds, our relationships, our finances—to every place where we allow the Prince of Peace to rule and reign.

The peace that this generation is longing for will only be found in seeing Jesus. It will not be found in self-help or hashtags or even in social justice movements; these things have no ability to bring lasting or true change. Because ultimately, peace is a person. Jesus is the One they need to behold because only He has the power to keep them in perfect peace.

Father, we thank You that You have promised to keep in perfect peace those whose hearts and minds are set on You. By the grace and power of Your Holy Spirit, we ask that You would turn the hearts and minds of this generation to see You and to receive Your gift: Jesus, the Prince of Peace. To their anxiety and fear, we speak, "Peace—Jesus—be with you." To their hurts and brokenness, we speak, "Peace—Jesus—be with you." To their minds, their hearts, their bodies, their relationships, we speak, "Peace—Jesus—be with you." Give them your gift of shalom wholeness today.

In Jesus' name, *Amen.*

—— SCRIPTURES TO PRAY ——

Isaiah 26:3
John 14:27, 20:19-21
Romans 5:1
Philippians 4:5-9

# 21
## HUNGER AND THIRST

*Beth Ferguson*

I watched a child run up to our pastor's wife to ask for a snack. He cut his eyes slyly to his mom, knowing that he was pushing a boundary. He also knew who the keeper of the snacks was and how easy it would be to get a tasty treat.

While I don't remember the last time I was hungry, it seems our children are rarely full. Our goal is to feed them nourishing foods while also fulfilling their desire for an occasional treat. So we read labels, search ingredients, and analyze nutrition.

As I shopped for snacks recently, I was reminded of our need to hunger and thirst after righteousness. *How do we create hunger in our own desires? How do we create it in the younger generation?* In a world filled with spiritual junk food, I have to prime my appetite, tending to the diet I feed my mind. As I become aware of my failings, weaknesses, and sin, my desire to know God increases. Reading God's Word, hearing it in church, and talking about it with others reveals my need for Him and leads me to Him for the life-giving nourishment my soul craves.

I long for the young people in my sphere of influence to run to God with their hunger! I want them to find satisfaction in His Word, to taste the honey, digest the meat, and grow up in Him so that they can be filled with His righteousness.

Father, we thank You that You created us to live in relationship with You. We ask that You will whet our children's appetites for You and guide us as we endeavour to model good, nourishing habits for them. Adjust their taste buds so that Your words are sweeter than honey to their mouths. Increase their desire for spiritual milk, and grow them up to enjoy the solid food on Your menu. Give them wisdom to set their minds on things above, hungering and thirsting after righteousness so that they will be filled with the measure of all the fullness of God. In Jesus' name, *Amen.*

—— SCRIPTURES TO PRAY ——

Psalm 63:1-5, 119:102-104
Matthew 5:6
Colossians 3:1-2
Hebrews 5:11-14
1 Peter 1:22-2:3

# 22
## ACCORDING TO YOUR WORD

*Aimee Walker*

I once paid my girls twenty dollars each to memorise a section of Psalm 119. One diligently chipped away at it, learning one verse at a time. The other resisted, then one night decided she needed money; by morning, she knew it by heart. While they had *very* different approaches, incredibly, they both remembered it all a week later.

The very first verse they memorised from the passage was this one: "How can a young person stay on the path of purity? By living according to your word" (Psalm 119:9). My heart fervently desires for my children to not only walk but to stay on the path of purity. But I know that for this to happen, they must choose to align their lives with God's Word. And for that to happen, they must first know the truth of His Word. They need to know what God has to say about who they are, their circumstances, and the world they live in. They need to know His ways, but more than anything, they need to know *Him*. The Scriptures help them to do just that because they illuminate the Living Word: Jesus.

We all know the lengths to which the enemy will go to keep us from our Bibles. He distracts and lies to us that it's no longer relevant or too hard to understand, discouraging us from opening the pages that have the power to teach, correct, transform, encourage, and sustain (2 Timothy 3:16; Matthew 4:4). My prayer is that the Spirit would awaken in this generation a great hunger for the Word of God; that He would give them the spirit of wisdom and revelation, opening the eyes of their heart to the hope to which they have been called.

Father, we ask that You place a longing for Your Word in our hearts and in the hearts of the children we raise and influence. We reject the lies of the enemy—time in Your Word is not a burden; it is an opportunity to delight in You and to receive from the storehouse of Your wisdom. Teach and instruct us through the Scriptures, opening our eyes to see the wonders of Your ways. When we don't understand, may Your Spirit instruct and guide us into all truth, so that we might freely and fully understand all that You have given us through Your Son, Jesus. We love Your Word; help us to raise a generation who will align their lives with its truth so that nothing will make them stumble.

In Jesus' name, Amen.

—— SCRIPTURES TO PRAY ——

Psalm 119:9-24, 65-72
John 16:13
1 Corinthians 2:9-12
Ephesians 1:17-19

# 23
## READY FOR BATTLE
*Adelaide Mitchell*

"All guys watch it" and "it's normal" are two common phrases passed around our culture in regards to pornography. Sadly, in this broken world, God's beautiful gift of sex has been distorted into a tawdry commodity which offers momentary pleasure that results in permanent damage. Particularly in the tender season of adolescence, when our children are beginning to experience the desires God designed them to feel, if they are not armed with the protective truth of what sex is meant to be, they may fall prey to pornography's destructive lure.

My three boys are still young, so we have yet to traverse this difficult ground. But no matter how much I yearn to preserve their innocence like a leaf untouched in amber, I know they will eventually encounter pornography in some form. My mama heart breaks at the thought.

Thankfully, there is good news. In his letter to the Ephesians, Paul details the protection available to God's children (vv. 10-18). When it comes to pornography, this generation is equipped by:

*The belt of truth* to recognise the dangers of pornography and how to avoid it.

*The breastplate of righteousness* to band together and live out their sexual purity proudly.

*The shield of faith* to thwart temptation and to remember that our greatest reward awaits in Heaven.

*The helmet of salvation* to remind us that, if we fall into sin, we are immediately forgiven upon confession and repentance.

*The sword of the Spirit* to actively challenge our culture's sexual norms before they can get close enough to take hold.

Sexual temptation is spiritual warfare—to pretend otherwise does our children a great disservice. We must make plain the enemy's schemes to steal their purity while helping them don the armour God gives them to remain steadfast in the battle.

Heavenly Father, we thank You that You have a good design for sex in our lives. We know that the battle against pornography requires both armour and artillery. We pray that You would enable us to have open, honest conversations with our children about its dangers, whether in our churches or our homes. We pray You would empower them to be strong in the maintenance of their sexual purity. Protect their innocent hearts, minds, and spirits so that when they reach the union of marriage they can enjoy the gift of sex as You intended. Lord, also help those who currently struggle with pornography to know that they are not too far gone. Thank You that even if they have engaged in sexual immorality, they can be washed clean, made holy, and accepted into Your Kingdom. In Jesus' name, Amen.

——— SCRIPTURES TO PRAY ———

Psalm 119:37
1 Corinthians 6:11-20
Ephesians 6:10-20
Philippians 4:8
1 John 2:15-17

# 24

## MAKE THEM HOLY

*Aimée Walker*


I grew up and got married at the height of the purity culture movement. While the motivations of this movement were good and sincere, it also did a lot of damage. As women, we saw our bodies as a 'problem'—something that could cause our brothers to stumble and sin. And so we became protectors for men, taking responsibility for both our purity and theirs, guarding our own bodies with heightened modesty, and 'saving' ourselves sexually for a future husband. Marriage became the end-goal, the finish line of our commitment to purity. For many, that goal fell short of our expectations. We questioned whether waiting was worth it.

Now, I watch my daughters navigate a hyper-sexualised culture with few boundaries. But make no mistake, the battleground is the same: holiness.

Sexual purity is part of our call to be holy as God is holy (1 Peter 1:16). Yet it is not intended to be a list of rules but a heart response to the price Christ paid for our freedom (1 Corinthians 6:20). It also isn't intended to be fixed on a single person or to be a source of shame; rather, the pursuit of purity is meant to be the pursuit of intimacy with God Himself, fuelled by an awareness of our great honour in housing His Spirit (1 Corinthians 6:17-19).

When Paul exhorts the church to flee from sexual immorality, reminding them they are temples of the Holy Spirit, the wording He uses doesn't describe the Temple generally; it refers to the Holy of Holies. Our bodies are sacred places where God Almighty has chosen to come and dwell.

We must believe for this generation to have a fresh revelation of who they are in Christ that they might steward their freedom with purity and thereby experience the intimacy they were meant for—with God and with one another.

Father, we thank You that You created us for intimacy—intimacy with one another and ultimately with You. We pray that the enemy would not be able to use sex as a source of confusion or shame in the lives of our children but that it would be the gift You intended it to be. Bring them to an understanding of who they are in Christ that they might use their freedom for that which is beneficial, honouring You with their bodies. Strengthen them to flee not only from sexual immorality but from anything that would hinder their relationship with You. Empower them to keep in step with the Spirit who now fills them so that they might become holy as You are holy.
In Jesus' name, Amen.

—— SCRIPTURES TO PRAY ——

Matthew 5:8
1 Corinthians 6:12-20
Galatians 5:13-26
James 4:8
1 Peter 1:16

# 25
## EXTRAVAGANT WORSHIPPERS
*Hannah Tan*

My second baby is almost four years old now, and he pours everything within him into passionate acts of worship, whether it's song and dance or service and compassion. It's beautiful but costly for him; his little body tires out from the physical exertion, and his mind is still growing in capacity for understanding. It's costly for me, too; as I allow him space to express his love of God and people, I'm also teaching him how to listen to and look after his body and soul in the process.

Despite the cost, though, worship is always worth it. I'm reminded of Jesus honouring the woman who anointed Him with oil (Luke 7:36-50). Her worship cost her dearly, financially and socially, yet her testimony of forgiveness and freedom is still being shared today. I'm also reminded of David, standing in the gap for Israel and being offered all he needed to build an altar to offer sacrifices, free of charge (2 Samuel 24:24), yet he insisted on footing the bill because he knew that worship must cost something to be worth anything.

For a generation that chases the quick fix, the fleeting trend, the easy, cheap, and shallow, I pray they would not see their Father God that way, but as their Saviour and worthy of pouring out their lives for—with joy and vigour like my son, with boldness and gratitude like the woman with the anointing perfume, and with a heart bent toward honour and truth like David.

Father, we thank You that You are worthy of our worship. Thank You for showing us what true worship is through your Word. We ask for boldness for this generation, that they would not shy away from worshipping You because the price is too steep. We pray that, like David, they would say, "I will not offer something that costs me nothing," but would daily die to self to honour You with their lives, even as small children. We ask that You would guide us as we teach and model costly worship with our own lives each day.

In Jesus' name, *Amen.*

—— SCRIPTURES TO PRAY ——

Deuteronomy 6:5
2 Samuel 24:24
Luke 9:23-24
John 4:23-24
Philippians 2:17

# 26
## FAITHFUL PARTNERS
*Aimée Walker*

"Meaningless, meaningless....Everything is meaningless" (Ecclesiastes 1:2). "Let us eat and drink, for tomorrow we die" (Isaiah 22:13 ESV). If my daughter was more familiar with the writings of Solomon and the prophets, these might have been the words she'd have chosen as she vented to me about the pointlessness of life one night. Overwhelmed by the complexities of the culture she is growing up in and the weight of her own issues, purpose felt out of reach; there seemed no reason to not throw off restraint and live it up.

I know she is not alone in her sense of despair and her quest for meaning in the face of uncertainty and suffering. We live in a time where everything that can be shaken, is; a time when it is vital that we understand that our inheritance is imperishable (1 Peter 1:4) because we belong to a Kingdom that cannot be shaken (Hebrews 12:28). It is the immovability of the Kingdom of God that brings meaning and perspective to every season under the sun.

No matter how hopeless the world feels, we can continue to partner with God to see it be on earth as it is in Heaven (Matthew 6:10). As God instructed the Israelites in a time of exile, we must teach our children to build houses and plant gardens and increase in number, prayerfully seeking the peace and prosperity of the lands God has settled them in (Jeremiah 29:5-7). As they are faithful to cultivate what God has entrusted to them, not only will they discover the meaning they are longing for, but they, too, will prosper and know the peace of God.

Father, we thank You that our hope is living; it is for what we find ourselves facing right now, but it is also anchored in the assurance of our future inheritance in Christ. We ask that no matter what this generation faces or where they find themselves that they would not despair but rather faithfully partner with You to see it on earth as it is in Heaven. Bless and prosper the work of their hands, and help them to discover divine purpose in the day-in, day-out tasks of building and planting. We declare that they will be a generation that prayerfully seeks Your face, that knows Your gift of peace and releases it to the world. In Jesus' name, Amen.

―― SCRIPTURES TO PRAY ――

Proverbs 14:34
Jeremiah 29:5-7
Matthew 6:9-13
Hebrews 12:28-29
1 Peter 1:3-6

# 27
## GRACE TO HOLD ON
*Aimée Walker*

I've been watching some of my kids wrestle with God of late. Wrestling with whether they trust His ways and His Word. Wrestling with whether they want Him to be their God—if He's even real. It's been hard for my mama heart to watch, and part of me has wanted to circumvent it on their behalf. But I know that this process is healthy and sometimes necessary if they are going to be able to wholeheartedly love and trust God for themselves.

Madeleine L'Engle writes, "Those who believe they believe in God, but without passion in the heart, without uncertainty, without doubt and even at times despair, believe only in the idea of God and not in God Himself." When we don't allow ourselves to offer up to God our questions, our pain, our disappointments, and our doubts, we keep God at arm's length and rob ourselves of greater intimacy. It is only when we learn to do our wrestling *with* Him rather than *apart* from Him that our battlegrounds can become a place of blessing.

In Genesis 32:26, Jacob physically wrestles with God, and he cries out saying, "I will not let you go unless you bless me." When our children grapple with God, we need to stand in the gap and ask that He would enable them to hold on to Him and not let go until their struggle has been overcome. And as they wrestle, we must trust that no matter how they are 'wrenched' in the process, our loving Father is able to turn it all for good.

Father, we lift up to You our children who are wrestling with their faith in this season. We ask that You give them grace to hold on so that their struggle can give way to the blessing of knowing and being loved by You. Help us to be transparent in our own wrestling so we can model for them what it looks like to bring our questions to You and find comfort, counsel, and truth in Your presence. Thank You for Your great love for our children, for the compassion and mercy You show them even as they wrestle. We declare, "Great is Your faithfulness." Reveal Yourself to them. In Jesus' name, *Amen.*

—— SCRIPTURES TO PRAY ——

Genesis 32:22-32
Lamentations 3:22-23
Luke 15:1-7
John 10:27-28

# 28
## SECURE IN IDENTITY

*Rachel Miller*

How popular would Jesus be on social media if He was physically walking the earth today? What would be the reaction to uploaded videos of miracles, profound hashtags, gatherings of thousands—and how would the world react watching His painful journey towards the Cross?

But Jesus did not desire or seek popularity nor did He need it. He understood the purpose of His life and ministry, and His confidence in the Father's love for Him enabled Him to faithfully live it out. But it wasn't always easy. We read in Matthew 4:1-11 that Jesus stood against Satan's temptations as He wandered in the desert for forty days and nights after being baptised; the temptation to accept the world's glory and approval must have been intense in His physically-weakened state. However, Jesus held onto the truth of His identity; all His glory came from being the Father's Son, given to Him in order that the Father would be glorified in return (John 17:1-5).

When we do not fully comprehend our identity as a child of God, we can succumb to temptation in many areas of our lives. Surrounded by the pressures of popularity, we are easily led away from the Father's heart, creating false and unrealistic expectations of ourselves and, ultimately, who we are created to be. It is only by clinging to the example of Christ and His refusal to give in to temptation that this rising generation can find true identity, approval, and belonging.

Father, today we pray for our children to understand the truth of who You are and who they are in You. Protect their hearts, minds, and souls from the world's temptations and any spiritual attack of deception on the core of their being; help them to discern who is speaking to and leading them and for what purpose. We pray Your voice would be loud, clear, and familiar to our children so that there would be no confusion in their minds. We ask, Father, that You would surround them with loving, God-fearing individuals through every season of their lives to remind them of their identity as Your children with whom You are well-pleased. Help us to raise a generation that is bold in their faith and identity and who live out of love for You.
In Jesus' name, Amen.

——— SCRIPTURES TO PRAY ———

Matthew 4:1-11
John 10: 1-16
Romans 8:38-39
Ephesians 6:10-18
James 4:7

# 29
## LIFT UP YOUR HANDS

*Aimée Walker*

In my mid-twenties, someone I loved dearly had wandered far from God. I'd been praying for them but somewhat passively. Then the Holy Spirit directed me to the book of Lamentations and used Jeremiah's vivid imagery of the destruction and exile of Israel to awaken something fierce within me. As I read of how the enemy had laid hands on Israel's treasures, entering the sanctuary, the place where they had no right to go (1:10), of how her children were destitute because the enemy had prevailed (1:16) and how her youth had been sent into exile (1:18), I saw how spiritually the same was happening now to a generation within the Church. Like Jeremiah, a deep grief for what was being lost entered my heart.

But it was these words that got me on my knees: "Arise, cry out in the night, as the watches of the night begin; pour out your heart like water in the presence of the Lord. Lift up your hands to him for the lives of your children, who faint from hunger at the head of every street" (2:19). I, and others, committed to regularly pray and fast for the prodigals within our church. Within weeks, the loved one I had been praying for recommitted their life to the Lord. We kept praying, and that year, several prodigals returned to the Father's house.

We cannot sit passively by as the enemy comes into our homes and goes where he has no right to go and takes what he has no right to take. Our children are our treasures and many of them are hungry, desperately searching for answers where they will find none. We must lift up our hands in intercession for their very lives—eternity hangs in the balance.

Father, we humbly come before you on behalf of a generation who has wandered far from your house. We lift up our hands and ask that their hunger be satisfied by You alone. Holy Spirit, turn their hearts back to the Father. Enable them to see how eager He is to lavish His love upon them. Stir their hearts that they might believe and confess that Jesus is Lord. We commit to standing watch in prayer, believing in faith that our homes and churches will be places of salvation and all who enter into them will give you praise for your faithfulness. We declare that no longer will the enemy prevail, but we and our households will serve the Lord. In Jesus' name, Amen.

—— SCRIPTURES TO PRAY ——

Joshua 24:15
Isaiah 60:18
Lamentations 2:19
Matthew 19:25-26
Romans 10:9-10

# 30
## PROVIDE A WAY OUT
*Aimée Walker*

"Because I said so." It's an age-old parenting line that we like to pull out when our kids are questioning our instructions. When they're younger, often our word is enough to put an end to the discussion, but as they get older, they want to understand the 'why' for themselves. They start to push back against us, testing the boundaries to determine whether they agree with our decisions and reasoning—and what they're going to do about it.

They do the same with their faith. "Because the Bible says so," often isn't enough as they grow, either. Just like they want to know whether their parents' wisdom is worth following, they want to know if God's is, too. This can be a healthy process, a time when they put down roots and begin to own their faith for themselves, moving from religion to relationship. But it can also be a time of temptation where boundaries are tested as they become vulnerable to peer pressure and the opposing ways of the world. Fortunately, there is a way for them to get the help they need: prayer.

When Jesus taught the disciples to pray, He instructed them to ask: "Don't let us yield to temptation, but rescue us from the evil one" (Matthew 6:13 NLT). Hours before His crucifixion, He reminded them again to pray they would not fall into temptation (Luke 22:40). We must follow the model Jesus has set for us, interceding for this generation to be able to withstand the many temptations that come their way. But we must also teach them that the power of prayer is available to *them*—that they can cry out to the Lord, and He will be faithful to provide them a way out.

Father, we echo the words that Jesus taught the disciples to pray: Don't let our children yield to temptation, but deliver them from the evil one that they might know in the depths of their being that Yours is the Kingdom, the power, and the glory. Holy Spirit, help them to check their desires against the standard of the Word. Help them to discern what is of God and what is not; give them eyes to see that You are faithful to provide a way out of sin that they might master it instead of becoming enslaved. May they walk in the freedom of Christ, willingly submitting to His authority and choosing only what is beneficial that their lives might honour You.
In Jesus' name, Amen.

—— SCRIPTURES TO PRAY ——

Matthew 6:9-13
Corinthians 6:12-20, 10:12-13
James 1:12-15
2 Peter 2:9-10

# 31
## GUIDE THEIR PATHS
*Nichole Gillanders*

Proverbs 22:6 tells us to "start children off on the way they should go, and even when they are old they will not turn from it." Unfortunately, it doesn't warn us that they may still wander. Whether we are a parent, grandparent, or friend, it is hard to watch youths stray from the path we so desperately want them to follow.

When my children were young, it was easy to correct them; I could help them choose their friends and steer them in the right direction when making choices. As they grow, however, I am finding more and more that I have to 'let go and let God,' releasing my grip on their lives so He can take the wheel. I struggle to step back, but if I want to secure our relationship, I know I need to become less in their lives so He can become more—or risk them resenting me.

In John 14:26-27, we read: "But the Advocate, the Holy Spirit, whom the Father will send in my name, will teach you all things and will remind you of everything I have said to you. Peace I leave with you; my peace I give you. I do not give to you as the world gives. Do not let your hearts be troubled and do not be afraid."

Because the Holy Spirit lives in me and my children, I can embrace the peace He gives me as He does His good work in our lives. I can stand confident in the knowledge that, as I encourage this next generation to walk God's path while they are young, He is faithful to guide them into the wisdom they need to stay on it.

Father God, we thank You that You guide our paths, and we choose today to submit to Your teaching. We surrender our expectations. We surrender our ways. We surrender our words. Use us as a witness to the next generation in a way that they will see Your light, Your love, and Your life. Draw them to others that will do the same. Give them eyes to see the truth, awareness of the deceptiveness of the world, and the discernment to know the difference. Let whatever is true and kind grow in their minds and come out of their mouths. Surround them with wise counsel. Give us the right words and actions to guide them on Your path so that they do not stray from it.
In Jesus' name, *Amen.*

—— SCRIPTURES TO PRAY ——

Proverbs 4:11-13, 22:6
John 14:26-27
Philippians 1:6

# 32
## COMMAND YOUR ANGELS

*Aimée Walker*

During a difficult parenting season, a girlfriend called to share a series of pictures she had seen while praying for one of our children. One of the images was of our child encircled by angels, and she felt led to encourage us that, while it might have looked to us like nothing was happening, God was actively protecting them. His angels were on the case!

Reading the New Testament, I'm struck by the prominent role angels play. From the opening chapters of Matthew's gospel where Joseph experiences two angelic visitations and Jesus is attended by angels after His temptation; to Luke's gospel detailing Gabriel's visits to Zechariah and Mary and the angel who strengthened Jesus before He went to the cross; to Acts where angels set the apostles free from prison, gave Philip guidance, and appeared to Cornelius in a dream, we see angels not only acting as God's messengers but also fulfilling their role as "ministering spirits sent to serve those who will inherit salvation" (Hebrews 1:14). And as I've pondered all of this, I've been deeply encouraged by Jesus' words as He taught the disciples to value little children: "See that you do not despise one of these little ones. For I tell you that their angels in heaven always see the face of my Father in heaven" (Matthew 18:10).

Our children have angels assigned to them—angels who are in the very presence of the Father. They are ready and able to do His bidding, working behind the scenes to see His plans for them accomplished. At any moment, these angels can be deployed on our children's behalf. All we need to do is ask.

Father, thank You that our children have angels assigned to them who are before Your throne and more than able to do Your will. We ask that You command Your angels to guard this generation in all of their ways, to encamp around them, to deliver them, and to minister to them. May the reality that the early church experienced of angels guiding and protecting also be the testimony of this generation. May they be aware of the lengths that their loving Father goes to to fulfil His purposes for them.

In Jesus' name, *Amen.*

—— SCRIPTURES TO PRAY ——

Psalm 34:7, 91:9-12
Matthew 18:10
Hebrews 1:14

# 33
## LIE DOWN AND SLEEP

*Aimée Walker*

When our children are first born, we quickly look forward to the day when they will sleep through the night. Strangers and friends alike share in this hope with us, often asking parents of new babies, "How are they sleeping?" But as our children grow, the question fades, and the assumption is that our no-longer-infants sleep soundly. Yet, as I've discovered, sleep does not always characterise the older years.

From night terrors to bad dreams to insomnia to anxiety about the day ahead, the night can become a time of fear and darkness for our children rather than the place of rest that God intended it to be. With the rise in mental health issues for children and adolescents, this is an increasing problem; our children are being robbed of the rest that is vital to their growth and sense of well-being.

God intended the night to be a respite from the activity and demands of the day, a place of refreshment and dreaming. He invites His children to lie down free from fear and to experience the sweetness of sleep (Proverbs 3:24). He wants to be what fills their thoughts through the night watches (Psalm 63:6) and His truth to be the source of instruction for their hearts (Psalm 16:7) so they awake refreshed and equipped for what the day will hold.

We need to reclaim the night and believe for God to grant sleep to these children whom He loves (Psalm 127:2) that they might know His rest and dream dreams of hope for their generation.

Father, we thank You for the gift of rest, and we ask in Jesus' name that You would grant sleep to Your beloved children. May Your perfect love cast out their fear and transform the night watches into a time of peace. Create in them an awareness that they are under Your care and protection—an understanding that You neither slumber nor sleep but continually watch over them. Instruct their hearts as they rest, tearing down the lies and arguments that keep them from truly knowing You. Send Your angels to minister to them, and by Your grace, enable them to dream dreams that will bring You glory and reveal Your goodness to this generation.
In Jesus' name, *Amen.*

—— SCRIPTURES TO PRAY ——

Psalm 4:8, 16:7, 63:6, 121:4-8
2 Corinthians 10:3-5
1 John 4:18

# 34
## BE THEIR PROTECTOR
*Alissa Coburn*

I remember clearly the day my oldest daughter came home from middle school utterly distraught because one of her friends was "cutting." I felt badly for her and prayed for her friend, but it felt like something far removed from me. A handful of years later, however, a phone call brought it home: a friend's daughter had seen marks on the thighs of another one of my daughters.

Thus began our long struggle with self-harm. The first time she came to me with tears in her eyes and a towel wrapped around her forearm, scared that she'd gone too far, is forever etched in my memory. Since then, we've experienced all the ups and downs associated with depression and mental illness: prayer, tears, a hospital visit, stretches of victory, heart-wrenching relapse, medication, and counseling.

My daughter has not fully beaten her mental health struggles. However, she is currently experiencing one of her longest periods of victory yet, and she's fighting hard to keep it that way—and I'm fighting right alongside her.

Mental illnesses like anxiety and depression are on the rise, especially in children and young adults. When our children struggle, it can be exhausting and terrifying because we feel helpless and out of control. It drives us to our knees, which is right where we should be.

God loves our children even more than we do. He knows the contents of their days, holds their lives in His hands and has since the beginning of time. Be encouraged: He can heal and protect them, and He can comfort and strengthen you.

Father in Heaven, we come to You in complete surrender. We are desperate for the healing of the hearts and minds of our children yet feel as though we're too exhausted to continue the fight. Help us to rest in You, knowing that You alone are God—our refuge and strength. Cover and strengthen our children with Your grace, mercy, and protection in the battles they are experiencing within and around them. May they know your love deeply as they lay each fear and anxious thought at Your feet, trusting You to fight for them. We praise You knowing that You are mighty to save us and our children, and that, through Your Son Jesus Christ, we have victory over the enemy.
In Jesus' name, Amen.

—— SCRIPTURES TO PRAY ——

Psalm 30:11, 46:1
Zephaniah 3:17
Philippians 4:6-8
1 John 4:4

# 35
## RESTORE THEIR JOY
*Aimée Walker*

When Jesus knew that the time was coming for Him to return to the Father, He turned His attention from the crowds to the twelve disciples. One of His concerns in these final hours might surprise you: joy. Three times in John 15-17, Jesus expresses His desire that His joy not only be in us but that it be complete. He knew that joy is no trivial matter; the joy He gives brings necessary, divine strength to our journey. This is why Jesus prayed for us to know a life that abounds and overflows with joy, especially in a world where we will have trouble (16:33).

Today, this promised joy is being stolen from a generation. Depression and anxiety is rife among our young people. Even before the pandemic, one in five teenagers were likely to suffer from at least one mental illness. Now those rates are even higher. But these are not just statistics to me; they are the personal battleground of one of my children.

Mental health is complex and requires a holistic response, but make no mistake, there is a spiritual component to this battle. There is an enemy bent on isolating our children to steal, kill, and destroy (John 10:10). But we serve a Saviour willing to lay down His own life to set captives free and share His joy—and we get to continue that ministry.

Young people suffering from mental illness can appear difficult, defiant even. Their coping mechanisms are often labelled as taboo within the church, and so they retreat. Don't let them. Reach out. Show them love. Fight for them to get their joy back by coming alongside in prayer and in action. Allow the light of Jesus in you to penetrate the darkness they can't find their way out of alone.

Father, we thank You that You sent Jesus to proclaim freedom for captives. Help us to continue His ministry that Your oil of gladness might be poured out upon a generation and the spirit of despair exchanged for the garment of praise. We thank You that You are near to the brokenhearted and save those who are crushed in spirit. May those who wrestle with the darkness of mental illness today be aware of Your presence with them. Give wisdom to the helpers you bring alongside them, send Your angels to encamp around them and minister to them. Enable them, by the power of Your Holy Spirit, to know the full measure of joy Jesus' death and resurrection has made available to them. Take them by the hand as You make known to them the path of life and fill them with Your joy. In Jesus' name, Amen.

—— SCRIPTURES TO PRAY ——

Psalm 16:11
Isaiah 41:10,13-14, 61:1-3
John 14:1, 15:9-11

# 36
## BUILD THEM UP
*Aimée Walker*

She wouldn't make eye contact with me, and I immediately assumed the worst. I thought perhaps my daughter was mad at me (again) or was avoiding me because she'd done something wrong. I pressed her for answers. That was when the tears spilled over, and she told me how much she was missing her best friend who had recently moved away. My heart ached for her, and I was reminded that grief is not a respecter of age.

It's easy to forget that children experience grief. We mistake their outbursts, silence, and anger for 'bad' behaviour, when the reality is they're hurting and often don't know how to manage what they are feeling. When connections are lost, milestone moments are missed, or stability and normality is turned upside down and inside out, we cannot expect them to just 'get on with things.' Grief needs an outlet; weeping precedes healing, and mourning must be present if it is to be turned to dancing (Psalm 30:11).

We must offer this generation the gift of grieving well, teaching them to lament, but most importantly, to turn to the Lord for the comfort they seek. The psalmists and the prophets laid out a path for us in Scripture; they came honestly into the presence of God to lay bare their complaints, struggles, and pain. Holding nothing back, they allowed God to sit with them and be their safe place and Counsellor. The Father wants to give this same gift of His Spirit to our children that He might build them up with His love, especially in moments when their hearts are broken.

Father, we thank You that You make everything beautiful in its time—even weeping and mourning. Give us the wisdom to recognise grief in our children and the compassion to come alongside them as they experience it. As we make space in our hearts and homes for lament, help us to show them that we do not grieve as those who have no hope. Help us to point them to You—to the One who turns mourning to dancing and transforms Valleys of Weeping into places where refreshing springs bubble up. Holy Spirit, be the solace they need. Protect them from seeking comfort in the wrong places and help them to find refuge in the Father's presence. Build them up, bringing strength, restoration, and renewal to their lives. As they come to know the God of all Comfort, may they then turn and bring Your comfort to those around them.

In Jesus' name, *Amen.*

—— SCRIPTURES TO PRAY ——

Psalm 46:1-3, 84:5-7
Isaiah 61:1-4
John 14:1
2 Corinthians 1:3-5

# 37
## TEAR DOWN LIES
*Aimée Walker*

My son had broken one of his favourite toys, and he was devastated. I was prepared for the tears of disappointment and even anger that followed, but I wasn't ready for the torrent of abuse he unleashed upon himself. "I hate myself," he sobbed. "I'm so dumb." Feeling like I had a front row seat to how the enemy heaps shame and condemnation upon us, trying to rob us of our true identity, I tried my best to empathise with him while also correcting the lie entering his mind. I spoke out the truth of who God says he is, over and over, until he eventually calmed down and fell asleep.

Ever since that incident, I've been burdened by the reality that these types of lies are being cemented in a generation daily; that the enemy is causing them to not only doubt who they are but to loathe themselves. They need a company of spiritual mothers to rise up and declare the truth over them: "You are made in the image of God. Nothing about you is a mistake; from the womb you were fashioned with intention. You are fearfully and wonderfully made, a unique masterpiece made by God Himself on purpose and for a purpose. God delights in you. He rejoices over you with singing—you make His heart glad, and He longs to restore you back to the fullness of who He made you to be. You are loved with an everlasting love."

The young people around us need to hear these things come out of our mouths— who God says they are—but they also need us to get on our knees and tear down the spiritual strongholds the enemy has been building around them so they can confidently live out their God-given calling.

Father, we come before You today in the power and authority that You have given us as Your children, and we take a stand against the lies of the enemy. We speak truth into the identity of a generation, coming against confusion, condemnation, and self-hate. In Your everlasting love and kindness, draw them to Yourself and allow their hearts to hear and understand the truth that they are fearfully, wonderfully made, Your own handiwork, fashioned to do good works and reveal Your glory. Let them find their belonging and purpose in relationship with You; let the blood of Jesus wash them clean and bring restoration and wholeness where there is brokenness. Let them know full well that Your works are wonderful. In Jesus' name, *Amen.*

—— SCRIPTURES TO PRAY ——

Genesis 1:27
Psalm 139:13-16
Zephaniah 3:17
2 Corinthians 10:4-5
Ephesians 2:10, 13

# 38
## HEROES OF THE FAITH

*Beth Ferguson*

My kids are fascinated by superheroes. They love reading about them, watching shows about them, and dressing up to pretend to be them. They compare the powers of their favourite heroes and invent powers of their own to fit their creative stories. I love to listen in while they play; they express so much creativity and joy in exploring the fantasy of being more than human.

As I read the Bible, I notice that God uses 'heroes' to accomplish His tasks, but they are always very human. The only superpowers they have are those that God gives them. Heroes in Scripture are deeply flawed, yet when they are submitted to God's will, they can accomplish much in the Kingdom!

The apostle Paul defines a hero in Romans 15:1-2: "We who are strong ought to bear with the failings of the weak and not to please ourselves. Each of us should please our neighbours for their good, to build them up." Heroes use their gifts and talents—their God-given 'superpowers'—to help others, shouldering their burdens.

As I watch my children play, I want to instill in them a desire to do good to all with their own godly superpowers: love, joy, peace, forbearance, kindness, goodness, faithfulness, gentleness and self-control (Galatians 5:22-23). I want them to know that, no matter what weakness they have in their humanity, God calls and empowers them to be strong heroes in His Kingdom.

Father, we thank You for loving us so much that the only true hero, Jesus, gave His life that we might know You. Thank You that Your Spirit is at work developing fruit in our lives, empowering us to be effective servants in Your kingdom. Reveal our children's selfishness to them, help them to repent, and lead them to depend on You for the development of good fruit in their lives. Teach them how to give themselves to others, to strengthen and lift up their neighbours. Help us to demonstrate Your definition of heroism well so that the next generation will grow up to be kind and compassionate, leading in service to others. Teach them to walk humbly with You, God, and to do good to all people.
In Jesus' name, Amen.

––––– SCRIPTURES TO PRAY –––––

Micah 6:8
Romans 15:1-2
Galatians 5:22-23
Philippians 2:1-4
1 Peter 4:8-11

# 39
## A GENERATION OF PEACEMAKERS

*Aimée Walker*

In today's cancel culture, the word 'toxic' gets thrown around with alarming regularity, frequently being attached to people, behaviour, and relationships. My children often use it themselves, and while there are indeed times where this label is warranted and they've needed to put boundaries in place or even remove themselves from relationships and environments, I'm careful to remind them that cancel culture is not Kingdom culture.

As believers, we are called to love our enemies, to pray for them, and yes, to forgive them (Matthew 5:44). We are called to walk in the opposite spirit of the world. We are called to the ministry of reconciliation (2 Corinthians 5:18), to be peacemakers (Matthew 5:9). Peacemakers do not avoid or deny the conflicts they encounter; rather, they confront them with grace and wisdom, and above all love, in order to bring healing and restoration to people and relationships.

As spiritual mothers contending for a generation to know and love the Lord with wholehearted devotion, we must pray for our children to learn to navigate conflict in their relationships in a way that honours God and all who are made in His image. We must pray for them to have a love that is not easily angered, one that protects and trusts and perseveres with those they walk with, believing for God to fill them with His wisdom and to enable them to live with an awareness of the richness of the grace they have received through Christ that they might extend it to others.

Father, we thank You for Your extravagant grace towards us—that You do not treat us as our sins deserve but instead crown our lives with Your love and compassion. Help us to model this same love and compassion to our children so that they might learn to walk in the ministry of reconciliation as Christ did. When conflict arises, Holy Spirit, empower them to rise above the snare of offence; enable them to wear love, bless those who persecute them, and forgive as Christ has forgiven them. Teach them to fashion boundaries with wisdom and grace, always honouring the immage of God in the people around them. Raise up a generation of peacemakers: sons and daughters who bear Your name and reflect the culture of the Kingdom they belong to.

In Jesus' name, *Amen.*

—— SCRIPTURES TO PRAY ——

Matthew 5:9, 43-48
1 Corinthians 13
2 Corinthians 5:14-21
Colossians 3:5-15

# 40
## FOR SUCH A TIME
*Aimée Walker*

I don't think anything has ever filled my heart with fear the way parenting has. It didn't initially. I was young, idealistic, and enthusiastic, and I had 'unicorn' babies who seemed to do everything the books told me they would. But after I experienced the grief of miscarriage, fear entered my heart in a new way when I became pregnant again and experienced bleeding.

God ministered to my fear through the words of David: "Yet you brought me out of the womb; you made me trust in you, even at my mother's breast. From birth I was cast on you; from my mother's womb you have been my God" (Psalm 22:9-10). I knew God was assuring me this pregnancy wasn't going to end like the last; but even more than that, it was a reminder that, ultimately, *He* holds my son and ordains his days. I clung to this promise with both hands, every day a lesson in entrusting myself and my child to our loving Father.

Now, as I navigate the tween and teen years, I find myself having to relearn this lesson. And as I do, I find comfort in another promise: "All your children will be taught by the LORD, and great will be their peace" (Isaiah 54:13). We are not alone in our responsibility to raise our children; not only is God's Spirit at work within us, He's at work within *them*, constantly teaching, guiding, and shaping them. Like the Lord encouraged Zerubbabel as he faced the enormous task of rebuilding the Temple, we build and rebuild this generation for His glory, not by our own might or power but by His Spirit. We are empowered for such a time as this—and so are they.

Father, we thank You that You do not leave us alone—that You strengthen and help us, upholding us with Your right hand and empowering us through the indwelling of Your Holy Spirit. Thank You that the fruit of the Spirit's work in us is not only peace but resurrection power. Open the eyes of our heart to understand this hope we have that we might parent and mentor from a place of rest, knowing that, just as Your Spirit enables us, He will also equip our children for the challenges they face. Soften their hearts and open their ears to hear and understand Your instruction. Be their God, and enable them to trust You so that they, too, might know Your peace. In Jesus' name, Amen.

—— SCRIPTURES TO PRAY ——

Psalm 22:9-11
Isaiah 41:10, 13-14, 54:13
Zechariah 4:6
Ephesians 1:18-21

# TOPICAL INDEX

## FAITH

RELATIONSHIPS

# IDENTITY

# PURPOSE

## CONTRIBUTING WRITERS

We are so grateful to every woman who has lent her voice to this project. We pray their words strengthen you to keep standing in the gap and raising a shield of faith for the rising generations. Connect with our contributors on Instagram, and read more of their prayers @thedevotedcollective.

| | |
|---|---|
| Bentley, Vicki | @purposeful_joy |
| Brand, Rebecca | @rebecca.brand |
| Coburn, Alissa | @alissa.coburn |
| Di Julio, Ellie | @elliedijulio |
| Ferguson, Beth | @beth_.ferguson |
| Gillanders, Nichole | @nicholegillanders |
| Gleaves, Kay | @homesteaderkay |
| Miller, Rachel | @rachmillernz |
| Mitchell, Adelaide | @thestoneandtheoak |
| Rodger, Rachel | @hint.holler |
| Tan, Hannah | @tanboardingacademy |
| Walker, Aimée | @aimeerwalker |
| Wood, Lori Ann | @loriannwood |

# ᵗʰᵉ DEVOTED
### Collective

Our vision is simple: to serve God with wholehearted devotion, fulfilling the command Christ gave us to love the Lord with all our heart, soul, and mind (Matthew 22:37).

We want to love God with all that we are right where we are. In order to do that, The Devoted Collective is anchored in three core disciplines modelled for us in Acts 2:42: devotion to the Word, to community, and to prayer. It is our heart's desire that, through committing to these practices with us, you will experience the richness of all God intends for your life as you come to know Him more intimately.

The more we know God, the more we can't help but love Him; and the more we love Him, the more we desire to serve Him. And that's what wholehearted devotion is all about.

CONNECT WITH US

@thedevotedcollective
www.thedevotedcollective.org